"Ronda Miller's poetry is explosive and exceptional. I especially like the personal poems about her life, both because she has lived things I have not and she describes even small portraits that have such colors and images that engender emotional response to her straightforward words. She says 'if you want to know a poet, read his words…until they become your own.' Ronda's words become your own because they have such beauty and intimacy. Like the 'Rare moments' she describes in a certain dance and relationship, Ronda's sensitive poems bring one in and make one dance along with the rhythm. I was sad to come to the end and immediately started again at the beginning. You will too."

Alan S. Kleiman, author of *Grand Slam*

"Miller's collection, *WaterSigns*, charts water's path for plainspeople—water in the aquifer, water in the clouds, water in the field ditches and in the bird's beak and in the mother's womb. In this way, Miller's collection is a celebration of life's true blood, and Miller gets the people and the flora and fauna of Kansas-country right, right down to the dew drops on grass blades."

Kevin Rabas, author of *Songs for My Father* and
Kansas Poet Laureate 2017-2019

"These are poems that snap open like a milkweed pod to release their seeds of visceral life, silky from the interior life, to bud and bloom again. The soul has a shell, a scream can be prisoned behind a smile, the Lazarus kitten can live again, and all those kinfolk places that passed away, it turns out, left us word in these poems. This is a poet who grubbed up earth from beside the house that burned, because she knew it was precious, but then, from such relics, built these celebrations. Drowning didn't stop her, family feuds, lost love, times of dislocation so severe she wanted to die—but instead, this seeker turned her troubles into songs for us."

Kim Stafford, author of *Early Morning: Remembering My Father, William Stafford*

"*WaterSigns* streams with wind and sun, small towns, and prairie sky. Here, there is a current of coyote bones, a legacy in an old woman's eye glasses, a whiskey bottle behind a barn. Ronda Miller's understanding of the natural world is real and never glossed. So too, her people live in a Kansas of the heart, one with the wind that buffets them, a poetry that runs deep with a melancholy longing for simple truth."

Al Ortolani, author of *Paper Birds Don't Fly*

"In this book of verse full of memories and transformations, one poem begins, "I found his wedding ring on the bottom / of a glass jar filled with pencil shavings." The story is compelling, and the music of the language is a solace. Join Ronda Miller in her third full-length collection *WaterSigns* as she creates stories that sing."

Denise Low, Kansas Poet Laureate 2007-2009

"Ronda Miller's new poetry collection *WaterSigns* is a hard testament to our rocky communion with nature, and with how the often violent, temperamental world darkens and shapes youth, adulthood, and beyond. Miller reminds us in sure terms of life's temporality, how even falling trees can 'steal the soul / and leave the shell' of what we know. 'I think of how much water / it takes to fill your body and mine,' she muses, always mindful. Even so, the poet knows that the natural world is deep down a balm, a 'place of safe retreat' where we can whiff pipe tobacco 'sweet as homemade fudge.' With her new collection, Miller has granted us a glimpse into her guarded heart, a treasure 'worth more than gold.'"

Tyler Robert Sheldon, author of *Traumas* and
First Breaths of Arrival

"Ronda Miller's latest book of poems, *WaterSigns*, is a search for healing: healing for her, for the ones she loves, for the rest of us who share this earth with her. There are poems here that flay us with pain, carry us from the edge of suicide, "breaking pretty little vases / ...for anything / with sharp edges," to the depths of a widow's grief, "I found his wedding ring on the bottom / of a glass jar filled with pencil shavings. / ...dumped word ashes onto my palm." But then there are poems that lave the blessings of holy waters over those wounds: "You went all the way to the moon and back. / I saw you there myself," she says to a child awakening from a nightmare. "Touch Me with Your Night / and I'll show you my days," she offers, and you stretch out your hand. You would do well to accompany her on this search "... to... /find a sky where geese, / by instinct, / know where they are going, / and so do I." These are poems that seek words to help us come to terms with all that life presents, and in the end, finds them."

Roy Beckemeyer, author of *Music I Once Could
Dance To* (2014, Coal City Press)

WaterSigns

Poetry by

Ronda Miller

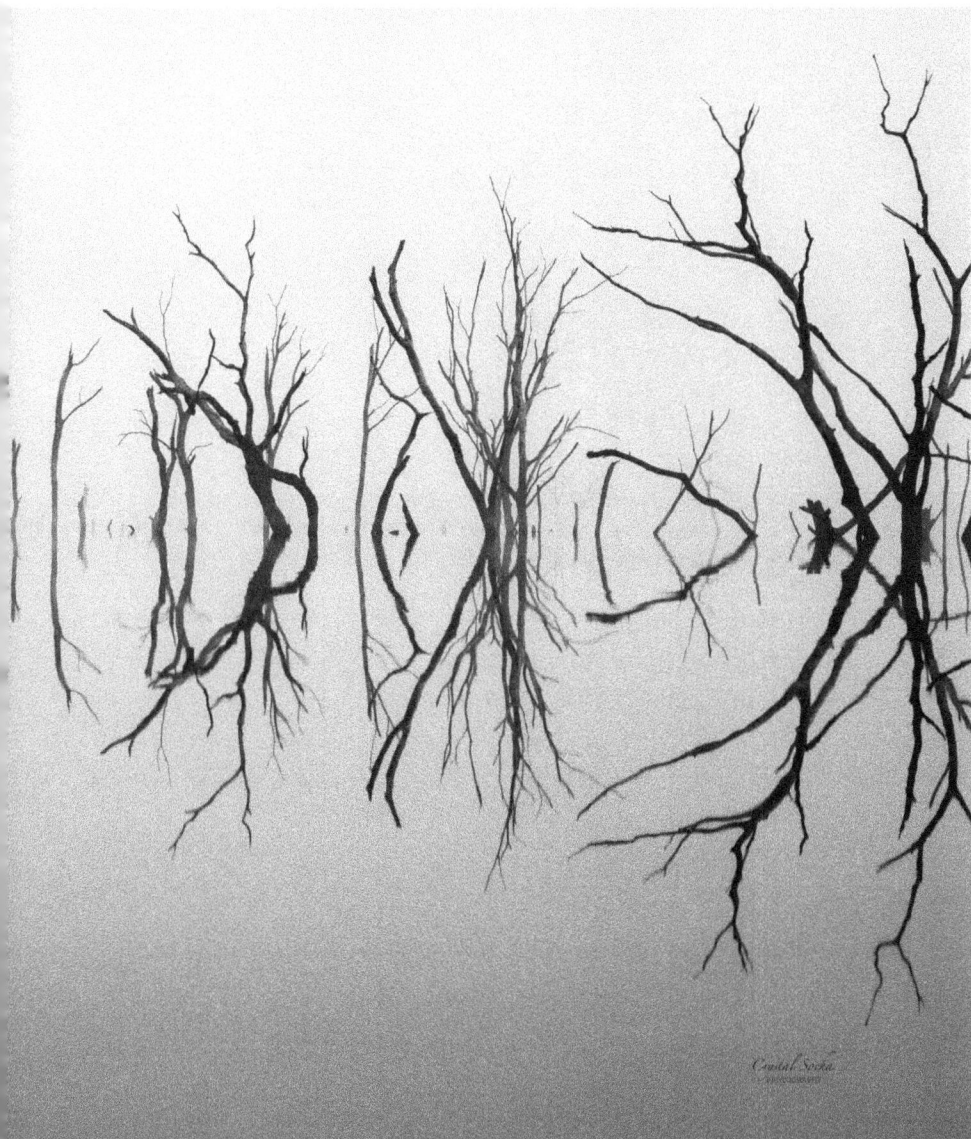

Coastal Socha

WaterSigns is dedicated to the people who stand for the preservation of clean water the world over, to those who appreciate that emotion flows like water, and to those who share water and emotion in innovative ways. When I met my father in my early twenties, following fifteen years of separation, he shared with me that he wished he would have known more about water signs in terms of horoscopes—in particular, Scorpio. He felt it would have made a difference in my mother's suicide. He and my mother and I all share the Zodiac sign of Scorpio. I offer this information only because it comes to me in these final moments of putting this manuscript together. Water is life's blood. I've always understood that deepest pool of unification.

I thank my family and friends for their support. In particular, poetry I've written about shared family members when memories and experiences differ. My children and my siblings are my life: Jena and Vernon Acors, Scott Wiggins, Scott Shreders, Apollonia and Gabriel Racca, Sasha and Jennifer Shreders, Nick and Julie Shreders (baby boy Shreders). I am thankful to have reconnected with siblings Jameson, Roberta, Yvonne, Carol, Penelope, Vanessa, and Calvin. To the following people who are no longer with us, but have never stopped drifting through my dreams. I thank my father Gerald Wiggins, my mother Peggy Miller Wiggins, Grandmother Helen Miller, aunts and uncles Earl and Glenna Neville and Doris and Lee Amsberry. They all had enormous influence over my young life. My writing career has been greatly encouraged by Uncle Dillard and Aunt Sue Wiggins. I also add two huge loves in my life, Sorrel Wiggins and Dimitry Shreders.

I don't write poems,

they right me.

~Ronda Miller

Meadowlark (an imprint of Chasing Tigers Press)
meadowlark-books.com
P.O. Box 333, Emporia, KS 66801

Cover and Interior Photos by Crystal Socha
fineartamerica.com/profiles/crystal-socha.html
facebook.com/crystalsochaphotography/

ISBN: 0-9966801-2-8
ISBN-13: 978-0-9966801-2-7

Library of Congress Control Number: 2017910248

Water Signs

Poetry by

Ronda Miller

A MEADOWLARK BOOK

Contents

WaterSigns

I flow in and out of sleep
like steeped, seeping water
from my mother's womb.

Tepid, swirling
movements below,
beneath a guarded heart.

Sights black,
sounds muffled,
scents and senses
underdeveloped.

A birth into blood,
broken particles,
fragmented consciousness.
Nude limbs flail and
swing as a first attempt
to swim into existence
makes a wide open
gasp toward survival.

Tossed upon parched,
wrinkled skin,
exhausted from heaving,
I become this fish out of water,
arrive in this new world
where retaining and remaining
water begins a lifetime of struggle.

Aquifer

A Quieter Kansas

The silence of cornfields
lulled us into thinking we'd never
grow old, leave the countryside,
send a son or a daughter to war,
bury a husband or a wife.
We had time to taste earth
muddied from an early morning
thunderstorm, lick syrup out of bowls
filled with freshly fallen snow ice cream.
We cracked marbles to make
necklaces for Christmas gifts,
pulled bloodied newborn kittens
from a heaving mother's
sides in the basement
of the one-room schoolhouse
that bordered the Kansas and Colorado line.
This is where we played spin the bottle,
stole a first kiss, learned to cook,
heating up leftovers sent from home.

On quiet days, we laid in the grass,
watched clouds wave as they angled
their way across the lightest hue of blue sky.
We straddled the Shetland pony bareback,
clung with fear and excitement
as knees pushed hard against his flank.
His tangled mane blended,
entwined with our own just as wild.

Hot Kansas days found us sweating,
toiling at play, climbing hills,
descending into valleys,
poking sticks into prairie dog holes,
scavenging the bottoms of creek beds.

We didn't carry a water bottle or lunch.
We accepted thirst and hunger as we accepted
the sun blistering our noses and our necks.
We didn't ask questions about the decaying
body of a coyote, ears missing,
cut off by grandfather's pocket knife.

We were children,
caught up in each moment
as though it was our entire life.
We laughed loudly,
wailed when we cried,
were dead to the world
when sleep finally came.
We didn't feel the sear
of overused muscles or growing pains.
We didn't hear the sluggish squeal
of the water tank
as it pumped fresh water.
Nor did we hear the howl
of the wind as it escalated
throughout the night,
slowly, but with certainty,
bringing change.
It was a time away from time.
It was a time of quiet in Kansas.

Above the Kaw

What spiritual message
from swoop to dive above
these frothy waters,
as you cry in victory,
do you bring in beak or claw?
Prey within thou neb silences
some while others speak
in native tongue and awe
of thou divine being;
an inspiration to a nation
for protecting young
soaring high above
the rest of humankind.

You do not reside among the living,
but in highest bough of tree
above the Kaw where illumination
lives inside your nest with squirming young.

Man, who dares not disturb,
waits and watches from afar,
detailing your every move
in hope a lone feather may fall;
a treasure worth more than gold
for his awakening.

Ronda Miller

Geese

circle around,
fly backward,
fail to synchronize,
flail and squawk,
eventually fall
into place,
their time and space
as confused as my own.

This year an antichrist
strides, legs long enough
to reach Kansas
from D.C.,
or is that New York?

Native Americans fight
for clean water rights
the world over,
stand their ground as
others shrink and shirk
family duties.

I keep faith/presence
with like-minded people,
promise myself
to continue the fight,
find a sky where geese,
by instinct,
know where they are going,
and ... so do I.

Just Dirt

I arbitrarily clean;
a Ziploc bag of dirt
shifted from one place to another.
I think about pouring it inside
a glass jar, ideally antique,
from the same farm
the dirt came from.
I think about tossing
it inside the trash bag
draped over an arm.
I can't bring myself to relinquish
that which brought me to my
knees the last time I visited.

The old homestead burning
to the ground was more than
I could bear. I clawed dried
earth, filling the bag, my lungs,
with what I'd come to love as a child.

My first real home.

It was the same dirt I craved and ate
following Rocky Mountain thunderstorms
that carved pathways through pastures and sky,
leaving my view and breath fresh, quickened.

I no longer search for happiness.
I accept emotions flow
like dirt through my fingers.

Water Marbling Kansas

New term, old art,
predictable images of times past
float as photos through my mind.
Switch out one, insert another,
no lack of them pulled forward.

Water . . . marbling.
Water . . . marveling.
Oily duck feathers,
water rolls off a back.
Marbles spin in water.
Attempts to shoot them under,
shoot them back to the top.
They glisten under white, blinding light,
wink their way out of sight.

I exaggerate.
Water marbling,
the art of laying colors down
upon different surfaces that don't mix
like male/female species skating on ice.

Mix it up, color it up,
draw lines throughout,
dissect, such an art.
I want to be above it all,
hold a wire,
power in my hand,
drag it across the sky of Kansas,
varied soil below.
Combine earth with sky.
God, the colors, the blend,
the art you have created.

Harvest

My sister and I climbed,
scraping shins along the way,
far into the upper branches
of the tree in my grandparent's
front yard that summer.
We could see pastures,
cows with heads bent to earth,
grazing,
the sky, an unbroken view.

We watched for signs
of dust puffing toward
us from the thin road,
winding miles ahead.
The one that took
us to Highway 36
on the school bus
or to our Saturday grocery
shopping in town.

We were in that same tree
the first time we met High.
He ambled through the gate
I practiced jumping over
and stood nearly eye to eye,
matching our height
in the tree branches.

His smile was broad and
we took an instant
liking to this stranger.
He lifted us down,
followed behind as we threw
open the screen door
to where our grandmother stood,

apron adorned,
in a standard farmhouse kitchen.

My sister and I were excited to learn High
would be staying for the summer harvest
and working on repairs needed for the granary and barn.
He slept in a twin bed in the room next to ours.

It would be the room my grandfather moved
into years later when arguments
with my grandmother grew more frequent.
High found time to play with us daily,
always sharing a quick wink and a broad smile.

We saw him early August at the county fair.
He spoke with my grandparents,
hat in hand, his gaze earnest and direct.
My sister and I watched from atop the Ferris wheel.

High waited to say hello,
to lift us down.
It was a month after wheat harvest
when grasshoppers and crickets
lay still from the dry heat of summer.
It was a month after my grandfather
fired him for drinking behind the barn.

Sage

I stood at the edge
of the Arikaree Breaks
and let the winds
of the world rush over me,
felt them push and pull
my hair in the heat
of this newly birthed
August day.

It was there I whispered
to William Stafford,
"Can you help me, Bill?
Can you show me a sign,
offer some words of wisdom?
I'm having trouble making
things right inside
my world, this world."

I pictured him
beside me, his calm
face pointed toward
the horizon. Perhaps
his eyes were taking
in the dew that had
gathered through
the night and sparkled
upon the sage that
smelled of both
heaven and earth.
He closed his eyes and breathed
inward with all his senses.
I was grateful to have his presence beside me.

His expression didn't change,
his mouth didn't move,
but I heard his voice on the wind,
"Be silent and listen.
It is all you need of today."

Cherry Creek

breathes the long slow
linger in goodbyes,
burning embers by a fireside.
Cheyenne county backroads
float in my rearview mirror.
The dust is strangling me,
I'm getting' the hell outta here!

Cherry Creek Valley remains;
my childhood never the same
with its infused
beauty running through
my veins. I long
to be home again.

A ball of twine,
two-headed calves,
rattlesnake rattlers,
Arikaree Breaks,
and caves with bats.
I catch a ride
on a flatbed truck,
travel I-70 like
a wounded snake.

I make my way in and out
of salt mines and quarries,
a museum in Hays
shares dinosaur days,
a fish inside a fish.
I get a mug of beer brewed
on the great, flat plains.

Cherry Creek Valley remains;
my childhood never the same
with its infused beauty
running through my veins.
How I long to be home again.
But home remains as mirage,
floating in my rearview mirror.

Ronda Miller

Confluence

Winter Meets

February came
for a visit this morning.
I saw him in discourse
with November.
They stood outside
my garden gate,
his fingers lingered
on her waist.
They gazed into
each other's eyes,
mouths moved in unison.

She comes each fall
to bring brittle, broken bones,
crumbled leaves. Takes hope
of love wrapped in a windblown
gown of browned Asiatic lilies
and chrysanthemum.

He arrives late winter
to view her acts of despair
and destruction.
What has been done
he cannot undo,
but he changes the memories
of that experienced firsthand
to leave hope of bloom
and life to come.

I'd never seen them together.
Perhaps they meet more
often than I know.
Perhaps they meet
when I'm asleep
in falling snow, thigh deep.

Trees

from my youth
blew hard and fierce
with a crack
and a break
as limbs
like family members
flew by,
bore bruises,
disappeared.

Wind wailed,
beseeched
with warnings,
"Don't take your
eyes off the giant oaks,
and cottonwood.
They will fall,
strike you down!"

Windless twilights
left them whispering
against the night sky.
I could see them
grabbling, grasping
at each passerby.

They'd steal the soul
and leave the shell.
A sudden goodbye
without a cry,
just the foul smell of death.

Morning light found them
clasping hands and sneering
as I watched, terrified.

Ivy Berry

Maybe it was an ivy berry
the kitten ingested
that caused it to go
into a coma or trance
so deep we thought it was dead.

My cousin and I placed
it in a Keds shoebox.
They, the shoes,
were the color red.
They matched the berries
we found nearby.

We used them to decorate
the head of the still, closed-eyed cat.
The mother cat lay nearby,
apparently at ease.
Perhaps she knew more
than she was letting on.

She nursed a new batch of kittens,
oblivious to this dead teen.
My aunt and grandmother clustered
with my cousin and I.
We were a solemn lot.
We gave an extended eulogy.
Afterward, my grandmother
laughingly suggested my cousin
suckle the mother cat's nipple
to see how her milk tasted.

If memory serves me, he did.
The dead kitten began to stir.
We rejoiced in its new birth
or regaining of consciousness.

It was later that night
that my cousin
showed me a jar filled
with writhing bodies
of Granddaddy longlegs,
appendages pulled off.
I was in awe of how long
they lived . . . legless.

Fake Photo Smiles

Trained like dogs
we salivate, anticipate
the click of a shutter, phone,
whirl of video cam.

It is an American scam
to act happy when
feeling bad emotions,
holding them in
when shoulder to shoulder
with kin you can't stand.

Make believe, fairy tales,
for one split second
we look like we live
the American Dream.

Hold your breath,
inhale your scream
until you explode.

Grandmother Against the Wind

My grandmother wore
dresses in the summer.
I do too.
They are quick to put
on and easy to change.

She wasn't a prim or proper
lady-like woman, but I thought
she was beautiful. Her image
came to me today; she was
standing against the wind.

My mother and my daughter,
shared her tall stature,
slim frame, contrast of dark
hair against porcelain skin.

I must have been nine or ten.
It was a windy, summer day
like this one, when she
motioned me to
where she stood,
waving me in like
I was a wayward chick,
and she was the mother hen.

She pulled a dress
from the closet she
shared with my grandfather.
It was splashed
with red roses
in a bold print
against a green
leafy backdrop of white.

"This is the dress I want
to be buried in. Don't forget!"

She didn't sound maudlin
or sad. She returned
it to the closet
and went back to reading
her *Alfred Hitchcock Magazine*.

I don't remember the dress
she wore at her viewing;
I do remember her
"coal black from a box"
hair was dyed a medium brown
because her eldest daughter
thought it looked more natural.

*I've never seen a natural
looking dead person.*

I'm glad I remember
the dress she wanted
to be buried in,
even though it has been
almost thirty years
since she died.

My Drowning Year

I was 17 the year I almost drowned,
not once, but twice.
The first time I was in rescue mode.
A favorite cousin,
he was eight,
dove into a pool in Los Angeles
while his parents stayed out late.

Some baseball game.

I struggled to reach him,
struggled to stay afloat.
I used him as a buoy.
My life flashed like camera stills
in front of my tightly closed eyes.
I had flashes beyond my lifespan,
so I survived.

The next time was by design.
I had a better chance,
I was on dry land.
No one noticed I was flailing around.
I no longer felt the need to breathe.
Oxygen was not a part of me.
There were no flashes of life
behind or in front for me to see.
No sense of time or being.
No awareness, no nothing, nothing at all.
A quiet darkness, no thought, no needs.
Within my deepest recesses a living
seed began to grow.
I began to feel hope.
That's how I went on living.

Bus Trip – When I was Terminal

I was 19 when I finally tracked him down.
I'm talking about my dad. I was strung
out and held a desire to connect.
Two years previously a simple call
from him landed me in the ER,
then an institution for seven weeks.
How many times and ways can a
17-year-old girl behind bars,
all personal items removed, try to die?
I must have discovered them all.
A plead for a razor to shave my legs,
hoarded pills, jumps from tables,
breaking pretty little vases
and knickknacks for anything
with sharp edges.

Nurses and doctors were invisible
during sleepless nights.
Other patients and I played cards,
a game of who could stand a lit
cigarette longest against our arms.

I wasn't so heartless or lost
that I didn't notice
the struggle the paraplegic
gave as staff held him to force
medication down his throat.
He was more determined
to die than I had been.
I admired him for that.

My last day in, I was given a breakfast
of eggs, bacon and toast. He was given pie.
He asked me to swap with him.
I did.

Double Stuff Chicken

A family separated by death
and deception sits down to dinner
at the table of two grandmothers,
one at a time. They live in the
same small town, hang matching
curtains in dining room windows.
Would they laugh if they knew?
They have not spoken for years,
ignore each other while standing
in line at the grocery store.
They share three grandchildren,
and a whole lot more;
the heartache of sending a son off to war,
a love of gardening. Both came to
this small Kansas town from Missouri.
One rode a train as a mail order bride,
husband unseen. The other came
when she was sweet sixteen.

We make small talk as I shovel
food onto our plates, exclaim,
"This is the best fried chicken
I've ever had!" and mean it.
A couple of hours later,
a kiss on the cheek,
a heartfelt goodbye.
I go to my car, loosen my belt,
drive a few blocks to my other
grandmother's house,
heap my plate full with a repeat meal.
Without missing a beat, I say,
"This is the best fried chicken
I've ever had!" and mean it.

You are a Black Scarf

but inside my head
you are always red
from the blood
that was shed.

You speak to me
in a quiet voice.
I hear you internally;
incessant pleas of,

"Take me with you, please.
The concert you're headed
to is one I would have liked."

You don't match my outfit,
but I honor your wishes.
You've accompanied
me to many events
these past ten years.

We travel as one
to places of fun
such as weddings
and other things
like the funerals
of those we both
knew and loved.

They loved you, too,
just as I still do.
I'm an emotional mess.
I can't get over you.

We're tied up as one
in this black/red death.
Darling, you died too young.

Each Day

I fight my way into the world surrounding.
A daughter's face/son's laughter awakens
life inside I thought had long disappeared.
Mother's fragile ways and smooth
white skin strive to reel me in
as she beckons from her underground
world of moss and stone.
The musky smell among the leaves is strong,
yet sweet,
like chrysanthemums placed at her feet.

And I am so tired.

My niece's almond eyes lure me,
invite me to a game of hide and seek,
bittersweet,
across the universe.
Perhaps it is a game that never ends.

My father's hands were all that were left
to recognize as they lay by his sides
in the coffin I chose. Badly bruised knuckles,
surely, they were meant to be a lesson on
how important it is to fight my way alive.

Other voices whisper my name,
but here I remain.
Each day I fight my way back in.
I fight that which calls my name.

Her Glasses

Numerous years ago,
I put dibs on her china cabinet,
the one that belonged
to my grandmother,
but an impatient personality
caught my husband
and I buying our own
at an antique shop
in Perry decades ago.

He asked them to throw
in the wheat embossed table
setting for eight. Sold!
I waited, anxious to gift
mine to my daughter
when she has
purchased a house.
My needs and attachment
for material items diminish
each year, while nature astounds,
calls to me loudly.

The items left
in the dying room
were few.
I could have gathered
them the evening of her death,
eliminating the need
to return the next morning.
I blamed it on fatigue, my laziness.
In reality, I needed
to return to make certain
what I'd witnessed was true.
There were no signs of her physical being.
She was gone.

I gathered the cassette player,
the CDs of Como, Martin, Sinatra and Cole.
Two small containers, filled with dressing gowns,
a small hairbrush, a tube of hand lotion,
and her Charlie Brown Christmas
Tree were all that remained.

Her glasses hadn't been worn for a month.

Her son offered me her jewelry.
I declined. I looked at her glasses,
thought of the things she saw during
her almost 88 years,
the emotions she felt,
the books she read,
the faces of those she loved.

Her son asked me a second time,
"Is there anything of hers you'd like?"

"Yes," I managed to say. "Her glasses."

I picked them up and gently
placed them in my purse.

Her 26th Birthday, Her Golden One

I drive high on this life's journey,
a zillion thoughts going through
my head. Tires on uneven roadways
bounce in a rhythmic pattern that sounds like
popsicles . . . pop . . . si . . . cles . . . pop . . . si . . . cles . . .
before it changes . . .
absolution . . . ab . . . so . . . lu . . . tion . . .
ab . . . so . . . lution . . . and, finally,
solution . . . so . . . lu . . . tion . . . so . . . lu . . . tion.

I have a stream of consciousness
mental processing consisting
of Fellini and Dali, images
of rampant sex with strangers, present themselves . . .
thankfulness that today my daughter turns 26,
never thinking she could
or would since suicidal,
family genetics bet against it.
My mother's—her grandmother's—genes skip her,
but not my niece.

I must remind her to warn
her children, to talk to them
about the family curse.
But over dinner,
flowers in her birthday drink,
we share the craziest and
funniest things she did as a child.

She says she always knew
her 26th year would be her best.
I breathe a sigh of relief and remember
many of my fears remain, thankfully, inside of me.

Raindrops

She Says

she doesn't dream.
Each afternoon I ask,
hopeful, she as despondent
as I by her response.
Not of ponies, a unicorn,
white kittens?" I ply.
She shakes her head side to side.
Full lips whisper, "No,"
so quietly that I'm lipreading.
During the day, she shares her tears,
tells me how badly she misses her mom,
who lives behind bars,
her older brother, who has somehow
transformed into her baby brother.
She cries for him too.
They have different fathers.
His came for him; hers has not.

Today I don't ask her if she had a dream.
I know she did.
I know she does every afternoon and night.
They are nightmares filled with a loss so dark
they can't be shared in the light of day,
can't be spoken, cannot be remembered.
They are felt so deep inside that
there are no words to share.

I sit beside her, rub her back.
Her dark eyes open, flutter shut, reopen.
"Let me tell you about your dream," I say.
"You were riding a rainbow unicorn
with a fuzzy white kitten in your pocket.
She kept flashing her bright blue
eyes to tell you where to go.
You went all the way to the moon and back.
I saw you there myself."
Her face relaxes; she smiles.

Little Tykes

Sammy wants to brush my hair, but it is an excuse
to eat it. Hands surprisingly large for his age,
he leans fully into me, puts his entire face
into my hair, breathes deeply and takes
it into his mouth. "Eeew," the other children squeal.
"He's eating your hair! He's leaving slobbers!"
I remind him not to eat my hair.
"But it tastes SO good!" he says
as he takes in another mouthful.
He eats only peanut butter and jelly sandwiches,
cookies, Cheerios, and drinks milk or apple juice.

His new friend, who goes to the same school
in the morning, but is brought on a different
bus to my house at noon, is more limited
in his food choices. Brian eats dry Cheerios
and plain flour tortillas. Brian holds two rocks
in his hands, doesn't speak, but does scream
loudly often. When I wash his hands, I wash
the rocks before I give them back to him.

Sammy starts running through the yard,
tapping everything with the yellow Little
Tykes hammer I've been meaning to throw
away, stops long enough to put his arm around Brian,
says, "What's wrong, little buddy?"
before he begins tapping wildly
with the hammer once again.
He taps the 14-year-old Persian cat,
who looks more than irritated as
he moves quickly through the yard.
He taps my arm, heads toward my car.
I steer him in a different direction.

Sammy's father arrives to pick him up, asks,
"Did he have a good day?"
I lie and say, "Yes."
Brian screams more loudly
when he sees Sammy is leaving.
I remind him that he still has his rocks in his hands.
I pick up the Little Tykes hammer,
make my way around the yard
tapping everything,
listening to the different sounds
it makes, so new to my ears.

In Japan

Today I return to work
and the bright faces,
excited ears and eyes
of the children I teach
and learn from as we
reenter each other's worlds.

I'm crying; the recent
loss of an uncle brings
fatigue, draws emotion
from my exhausted being.

I've shut down emotionally
the past two weeks;
too many other things
to be done to allow
emotion to get in the way.

Not knowing what
the children have been
told about my absence,
I simply ask,
"Do you know why
I've been gone?"

Excited responses,
hands waving in the air.
"Yes! You went to Japan!"

I laugh. It feels good
to be among imagination
and simplicity.

I look forward
to researching Japan
so I can share the details
of my absence with them.

Unnamed
Inspired by "The Mother" by Gwendolyn Brooks

I felt the dumbing down to numb
from the Demerol.
The taste in my vein
went straight to my tongue
and onto my brain.
The flutter
in that which is small
remained above it all,
listening in,
hovering close by,
not knowing if it should stay
or say goodbye.

The sound I heard
was the flapping wings
of a hummingbird,
the breath of the wind
that is in all things,
large or small.
It sings,
still,
in the limbs
of discombobulated
things.

Close Their Eyes

How infrequently that is said
in this world of violence,
mayhem, terrorist attacks.
Media controls our thoughts.
Visions of death and dying
appear before us as frequently
as our child smiling
with the missing tooth, then teeth.

Do we notice them
growing taller,
gaining weight,
the hopeful smile
now turned upside
down as their shoulders
begin to droop?

So much white noise
surrounds, turn off the sounds,
turn away from manmade light,
pull out wires, trust your gut,
look at the faces
of the children around you.

Don't forget.
Tell them.
Close their eyes.

A Child Asks, What is Death?

I did not wish to answer the child;
I did not want to show how
uncertain I was, how I feared
the question, how I feared the answer
more. I did not want the child
to know how much time I spent asking
the same question without answer.

If only I'd been asked,
"What is life?" That I could answer.
That I could smile about. I could
walk with the child and point out
flowers, trees, the sky, rocks
and a multitude of examples.
We could go to mountains, valleys,
and the ocean. I could stay up late
with the child; point out constellations,
fast moving storms that rushed
toward us as we ran, laughing, for shelter.
I could show the child the certainty
and beauty of a sunrise. I could offer
a strawberry; show the seed of varied
plant, the egg of reptile,
the new birth of mammal.
I could kiss the child
and hug the child and say,
"This, this is life!"

I did all this for the child.
The child was silent.
The child looked into my eyes,
smiled, and said,
"Death is the opposite of life."

I began to weep,
and the child gave me comfort.

Among the Wild Primrose

and rattlesnake master she hunkers.
Her white, sleeveless t-shirt is dirty.
Sand burs reside in the cruelest of places.
Cheeks stained by dirt tears weave
a ragged trail of sexual abuse.
She remains hidden a long time
after the sun goes down;
hours after her grandparents' car winds
up the gravel road, makes its way inside
the garage attached to the red barn.
Her sister's voice rings out clearly, joyfully,
"We're home!"
She left hours before—her first prom.
She wears a peach formal;
it highlights delicate, porcelain skin.
She has no words to tell what happened
when her grandfather
called her to sit upon his lap.
He told her how ugly
she was as he touched her.
She was turned away from him.
Perhaps too ugly to be seen,
she became invisible.
She carries her ugliness.
throughout her life.
She's made aware each time
she's touched by any man.
The police officers she works
with call her cunt, dickless Tracy.
They stop by her house off duty hours
still in uniform.

She carries her sexuality as her value.
She doesn't wait to be approached.
She offers herself willingly to strangers.
It's what she has.
It's what she knows.
It's who she is.
Relationships flower,
short lived;
a wild primrose.

Gaia

for Valerie Bennington Vidmar

You call me Earth Mother,
ground me with love,
gift a desire to be a better
person, poet, woman.
I didn't baptize you,
adult child,
with water from my loins,
you arrived with no pain,
before or after thought.

You appeared as gift
like warm bath water,
the luxurious feeling
of contentment following
love making or riding across
the prairie on my favorite horse.

As Earth Mother,
I feel compelled to name you.
Every child deserves a name.
Which child did Earth birth
perfect and complete?

Is my name Gaia?
Did I consummate star fluorescence,
tines of golden sun,
eclipse with passionate night?
Did I birth you whole, in part,
alone? No need for Uranus
to bring me wine,
Pontus to massage my feet,
Aether to suckle my breast
in preparation?

Did Tartarus kneel
between my legs to catch
your descent from the heavens?

Tell me, or not, your name
that I might breathe you
in and out
of my antiquated frame.

I've Never Met a Muslim

I didn't like, never been
hurt by, but was married
to a Jew. We used to laugh
as I'd say, "I love, Jew."
That was before we went
our separate ways.
I fear for the baby, what
will become of her. Six
months old, left alone
with Grandma while mom
and dad shot 'em down,
down, so many dead,
so many injured.
America is afraid
of you, the unknown likes
of you, large and small.
What will become of you,
baby? Will the media
hound, track you down
years to come?
I want to put my arms
around you, run far away,
smother you with motherly
love. Could we get away?
Is there anyplace
we could stay?
I never met a Muslim
I didn't like, I've been
wounded, hurt bad
by a Christian or two.
But what about you, baby?
What about you?
What can we possibly do?

Tedi – Spring/2002 – Spring/2017

I hear your comings and your goings,
your meows of request, loud purrs,
quiet movements with scratching,
padded paws, ease of escape
from little hands that eagerly reach,
not wanting to wait a turn to touch
your soft beauty. Your elegant ways
melt hearts, brings out the best in all,
except the dogs.

I hear your comings and your goings,
you let me in, you let me out,
fill my bowl with water, any food
I request if I rub my bushy tail
against your leg or simply gaze in longing.
You bath me, sometimes dress me in goofy
costumes that please. You take
me in for shots and shaves.
I've grown accustomed
to your strange, human way.

I see you failing, I see you faltering,
your breath now shallow and quick,
still climbing stairs to follow routines
of play and outside time among
the sights and sounds of birds and cars.
You feel the breeze of the first day
of spring inside your safe haven;
a refuge on the porch.

I feel your hand upon me,
sense your sadness and your love.
I hear words of comfort as you carry
me against your chest to my favorite
place to feel the breeze in my fur.
I hear birds and children at play.

I hear you coming.

I know you're going.

Ronda Miller

Mirage

With Certainty

He was my fixation.
I was a means,
an end to his addiction,
induction,
an indication he was a liar,
a supplier of guilt and need.

We mish mashed in life's mosh pot,
that part of our human existence
insistently inconsistent.

We both wrote, wrought
with wrongs and wrong doings,
words were worded such
that we righted ourselves,
other's misdoings and misgivings,
made amends for our madness
and that of mankind's.

We drove each other wild with passion,
a classical understanding
that we were killing each other,
not softly,
but with certainty.

While he had his blood cleansed
from toxins, I packed my bags.
No note written, no need to,
the chapter had ended.
We both had numerous books,
some under submission,
others unwritten.

Ronda Miller

First

Even in boots and Stetson,
I had you in height.
Prom of '69, wearing black stilettos
and an upside-down Styrofoam cup
to lift my hair piled high on top of my head,
must have made me rather impervious.
Not for you, you ambled
up disguised as Dopey from
the Seven Dwarfs and
the cuddly dough boy
all rolled into one.
Cheeks and nose red as any Santa's,
a look you retained throughout your life,
even though at some point
the hair under the hat disappeared.

News hit hard on Facebook this afternoon.
A man dies the way he lives.
For you, a tractor accident,
run over by your son-in-law.
I can only imagine how he feels.
Our last words in June,
no one in our class yet deceased,
a quick hug, your wife close by.
You requested a poem,
I recited my signature,
"I am My Home."
You were always first at everything,
this, no exception.

I Cradle My Song

as you trumpet your sound.
I hear your pain each time
the refrain rolls around.

It happens again and again.

My spirit dips and dives,
strives to rise
above earthly skies.

My song, your sound,
wears life's sadness
like a clown's
falsely painted face.

Drum your soul,
let it abound.
Strum disappointment.

Envy arises from the melody
of life not experienced
and missed kisses.

The surreal expressed
by lips blown
against trombone.

i saw autumnal

colors
through
rain
smudged
windows
this morning.

flowers,
pink and yellow,
sold by vendors,
a pastel
of unnatural colors
in sharp contrast
of falling,
fallen leaves,
purple
orange
burgundy
and burnt greens.

i travel
into your arms
again.

the varied colors
of our skin
a ripened hue of love

as we turn our pink
and white bodies
inside
out
for each other
again and again.

The One

told me he'd chase me,
throw me on the ground,
do things I didn't like the sound of.
The one
cried in school
when his barn burned,
prized polled Herefords inside.
They were his 4H project.
The one
said it was a sin to burn bread.
Heaven forbid!
The one
told me the truth when I laughed
and said my Shetland pony
had kicked the bucket.
The one
let me cry on his shoulder
as understanding came.
The one
went into the blizzard with a stranger
to pull a car filled with a wife
and children to safety.
The one
didn't go home to his own family.
The one
was killed by the semi
tractor trailer
traveling
on an almost
empty road.

Green Tomatoes

Summer days, masculine muscles
across the way flex in hot sun as I pick
green tomatoes from a friend's bushes.
A dog barks a command,
"Notice her! There is a thief
in our neighbor's yard!"

I'm reminded of lazy summer days
years past when I had little
to do but sunbathe at a motel pool
frequented so often management
surely thought it was my own.

The group of deaf male mutes,
hearing impaired the proper
term these days, eyed me as I eyed them.
They made fun of me as I strode past,
self-conscious in a blue, one-piece swimsuit,
unable to meet their gaze.

They touched a nose, pushed it skyward,
as if I was too proud or conceited to talk to them.
In reality, they were as alien to me as I to them.
Their warm, handsome bodies emitted waves
of sun spilled pheromones that titillated, thrilled.
Neither side able to imagine a language
in which to communicate.

Spiderman Underwear, Oh, Man!

We leave our separate motel
rooms at the same time,
his a door closer to the exit
than my own. He is tall, lanky, tan.
His medium dark hair shaggy,
but not unbecomingly so. His exposed
muscled arms are covered in tattoos.
He wears a camouflage t-shirt,
green shorts, mid-calf black cowboy boots.
He turns, sees me wheeling my suitcase
behind me, comments,
"What a handy thing that is,"
as if they are somehow new to the market.
I comment on his outfit—that he's starting a trend.
He pulls his shorts open in front, shows
me he's wearing Spiderman underwear,
says he bought them at the Walmart located next door.
I am wearing a Jurassic Park t-shirt, bought
at Walmart too. I unlock my car.
He asks if he can come with me. I respond,
"Only if you'll drive." He affirms he would part
of the time, but that he has no driver's license.
I quickly enter my car, drive away.
My hair, closed in the door, waves limply
in his direction as I pull onto the highway.

Touch Me with Your Night

and I'll show you my days,
my fright of ordinary ways,
of dreams unrealized.

Blanket me in darkness,
make it cool and deep,
a place to lie down,
a place of safe retreat.

Cover me, unbroken sleep,
rest my weariness upon your lap,
that I might take
a most extraordinary nap.

Storms rustle high in leaves,
I remain untouched.
Embrace me in stillness,
let silence be felt inside.

Old friend darkness worms
its way in. The messiness
from outer now cleansed
from that within.

Lift from me, your night,
it is time for you to go.
I have things to do this life,
your weight a crushing blow.

Banish you? I shall not.
I'll beg for your return.
Your darkness seeping in,
replenishes my soul.

Missing Colorado

Deer moved through
the campsite during
the night while
we got our Rocky Mountain
high on. We could hear
tongues licking dew
condensation from our tent,
could feel their hot breath
as it came preheated
and foggy through dilating nostrils.

The early morning chill
left us nestled together
on a queen-sized blow up,
sandwiched between layers
of sleeping bags and quilts.

Stomachs that had been
warmed by a smattering of steaks,
potatoes, and coffee the night
before began to rumble.
We made love knowing
the stars were shining above.

Pine beetles had destroyed
the campsite trees, nothing
was left to obscure our flight
into the night except
a promise of eggs, hash
browns, and coffee.

We whispered in each
other's ears about
the marshmallows
we'd leave seared

and smudged on the grating
of the fire pit as a special
treat for the deer when
they returned,
once we'd had our fill
of everything.

Inverted Tulips

This morning, the Iranian
placed a note in Farsi
on a bureau close to my bed.
He put it there
so I would dream of inverted
tulips growing on sloped
meadows in a poetry based
culture. It smelled distinct,
heavy as testosterone,
almost as delicious.

Yesterday, I followed
a recipe for Mulligan stew,
directions given by
the homeless person
who passed me on the street.
He placed a finger to his lips
to silence me. I could smell
the ingredients on him,
and I had the money
to buy what I needed.

Last night, a note
discovered from the Navajo
mother. It had large loops,
like lassos capturing the sky,
scrawled across the page.

This night,
no longer content
with who I am,
I go in search
of foreign tastes.

Word Ash

After the fact, we learn what we should have
known as we search for words and signs of love.
Important things material to share with offspring
left behind; to mourn items that sit in a drawer.

I found his wedding ring on the bottom
of a glass jar filled with pencil shavings.
If I had not shared the importance
of what words meant to him,
I would never have looked through his pencils.
I dumped word ashes onto my palm
and cried as I slipped the ring on.
It is back with the one who cares,
and where it belongs.

I learned much about him and his ways.
His books were treasured like bricks of gold,
that's how he spent his days.
He read, thought, deciphered words
of great authors who went before,
never realizing his mind was better
than theirs or yours.
I'd have told him if I'd known.
He would not have believed me,
an eyebrow raised.

I found the bag of pot buried
within the soil on his deck facing east.
His youngest son, our son,
took it there to ease his pain.
We watched our last sunrise,
he and I.
Then I told him one last lie—
that I lived with him again.

Reservoir

Ciao Bella, God

That was it,
"Ciao Bella, God,"
one of his last posts Sunday.
That and Elvis was a pimp.
I'm going to focus
on the positive.
He bled out last night
leaving his ex-wife,
a close friend of mine,
and two young adult children
behind to reel and wonder.

A life of waste is a wasted life.
There is much I can say about alcohol.
Self-medication, a brave choice
this lifetime, ultimate growth.
What the hell do I know?

Life seems normal this morning.
The dogs I walk, calmer than usual.
I suspect Paho is medicated.
Geese fly overhead,
a penny drops from my pocket,
a plastic wrapped newspaper
rustles underfoot, no startle reaction.

I'm calm this morning, emotionless,
aware that the next few days
will bring havoc and heartbreak
for my friend, their children.
I think of him, the way he went out,
no one could stop the bleeding.
Today is St. Patrick's Day.
He would have loved the party.

Night Noises

I've recently taken to leaving
my bedroom window
open several inches,
allergies be damned.
The phrase "creature comforts"
has taken on new meaning.
These sounds, the night
noises of crickets, toads, coyotes,
foxes filled with primal urges to mate,
the stirring sounds of foraging,
life and death sounds,
bring relevance
to my daytime movements.

I reconnect with nature
during the nights to be able
to make it through my days.
I imagine myself opening
the window by my bed
an additional inch each
year, until
I find myself on the outside,
listening to sounds of a family within,
instead of struggling to hear
the ones outside
where I belong.

Eliminate

Use it to describe refined sugar,
coffee, or animal protein
I removed from my diet.
It works for exercise,
although I don't have
it to eliminate anyway.
Use it to discuss a policy
that won't work, a police suspect
who has been ruled out,
or a boyfriend
I no longer wish to date.

It works for the red dress
left at the store because
it doesn't fit right.
But let's not use it to describe
the person dying in the street,
the one a government or police
state threw a weapon in front
of as an excuse to watch them bleed out.

People die, their souls leave their bodies,
travel to a different place
or hover around a mourning dad
and mom to comfort them.
People aren't eliminated,
human life is too precious
to equate it with taking out the trash.

Still, I Wait

Cries for help heard
over excited talk, laughter.
A new home, two small children,
acting grandparents here for the week.
Then, the rescue!

You'd gotten yourself up a tree,
no ladder, perhaps it had fallen.
Neighborly neighbors performed
daring rescue efforts,
nervous chuckles as names
were shared with manly
handshakes once your feet
touched the ground.

Summer nights I smelled
your pipe tobacco waft
onto my patio smelling
as sweet as homemade fudge.

We enjoyed nudging
with a joke when we met in public,
a wave across yards
over decades of shared mowing,
kids playing too loudly—then grown,
moved on and out.

I didn't speak to you
that last time at the store.
You didn't see me as you
made your way down
aisle number three,
so I slipped away.
I could tell
by your stooped form

and gray complexion
you were not well.

I bypass newspaper obits,
too many familiar names
on the list,
another just this week.

Neighbors told me of your passing.
I would have come
to your funeral, you know,
or at least have written you a poem.

Instead, here I sit. Still, I wait.

I Wash

the news down with pineapple
juice this morning,
it being less acidic than orange,
hoping to get it down in one gulp.
I suspect I'll be belching
shootings and lootings
the remainder of the day.

I watch clouds pass overhead.
A serene Kansas sky helps
take my mind off an ocean
of people washing ashore,
starving and dying
from any number
of preventable diseases.

I do what I can to go on living,
knowing my death won't
help them in any way.
They sit with me.
I sit with them.
Then we all go about our day.

Don't Get Attached

to those earthly things,
these earthy things, those earthly things.

Don't get attached to diamond rings,
butterfly wings, kings or queens.
Don't get attached to trees and leaves,
bugs and wind, song and rain.

Don't get attached to fire and smoke,
sticks and stones, hugs and pokes.
Don't get attached to laughter and jokes,
sleep and dreams, cake and ice cream.
Don't get attached to dance and dog,
song and romance, to cries or blues.
Don't get attached to hummingbird hearts,
to anything arts, songs to sing.

Don't get attached to rhythm and rhyme,
to sunset/sunrise, to the change of time.

Don't get attached to those earthly things,
these earthy things, those earthly things.
Don't be afraid of this dying thing,
this loving thing, this living thing.

if you want

to know the city,
squat and piss over
a manhole,
follow where
the rivulet spills
beneath jaded, neon lights.
go deep into its bowels,
place your lips against
veins as it sleeps
in alleyway trash bins.
blow it back into existence.

if you want to know the country,
place a cricket in your mouth,
savor the reverberation
as you rub your legs in climax.
give the stallion his head,
close your eyes,
trust his gallop along the v
of the gravel road,
will take you some place
you have always wanted to go.

to know a man,
don't go with him to prison,
look into his eyes, make love,
echo his cries,
rock him as he weeps
the tears he's held inside.

to know a woman,
watch her nurse her newborn,
look at her expression
as she reads the last page
of a book,

note the way
she walks
as she walks
away.

if you want to know a poet,
read his words.
do not trust you have
a clue as to what he meant.
read his words again
until they become your own.

Kindred Spirits

I met him on the dance floor,
like-minded spirits who
live as introverts—until
the music starts and
involuntary movement takes over.

For him, a few beers required,
for me, music is a contact high.
We smash, we clash buttocks
and breasts against each other
to the beat, imitate each other's
movements in twin mirror fashion,
laugh, make funny remarks
about ourselves and others,
his wife watching from
the sidelines over the years,
sometimes dancing with him,
with both of us.

Rare moments,
when I am in a relationship,
he smiles from a distance,
wishes me luck by blowing
kisses, gives a quick bump
when my partner's back is turned.
I contain a laugh, the urge
to bump him back,
my eyes plead with him to stop.

We sit beside each other
Saturday night, share
creative passions,
mine poetry, his painting.
He tells me he has had
no formal training,

that he began painting
nine months previously,
that he paints on cardboard.

He shows me photos
of his work. The next day,
my brother offers to buy
all 70 of the works
he'd never told anyone
about before last night.

After Midnight

trains whistle, wander
through recesses of memory.
A lonely existence barreling
through fog encrusted night,
a blizzard of white;
the train makes its way into sight
sometimes quickly as surprise,
other times with slow, stealthy moves
like the hand of an experienced lover.

I never gave them much thought
until I stood in the lunch line beside the senior.
I watched her face,
coveted her eyelashes,
for signs of her loss not dissimilar
from my own years past.

She hummed,
"After midnight,
we're gonna chug-a-lug and shout.
We're gonna cause talk and suspicion.
Give an exhibition.
Find out what it is all about."

Her father stood on the track
of our small-town train the night before,
let the hurtling black bullet blast him down,
but not one sign on her lovely face
betrayed what she was feeling.

Immure

Today I feel malaise.
I falsify the northern light,
the morning light,
in fact, all light.
I draw the curtains
to immure myself

in darkness.
It is only right.
For that which
my mind has forgotten,
my body remembers.
A time of broken hearts,

a knowing of unease,
an impending doom.
I place the blame,
a barbwire crown,
upon my mother's tomb.
It suits her well.

We Stand

I turn on the water faucet.
Not a day goes by that I don't
think about how blessed
I am to have running water,
clean water, water to drink,
to cook with, to wash myself
and my clothing, to flush
what my body can't use
away from me.

we refused them
the last few drops
of water knowing
it was all that was
keeping them alive

I think about how much water
it takes to fill your body and mine,
and how it flows through us without
our thinking about it.

how much longer
it would have added
to their hearts' beating
we had no way of knowing

My dreams are of Water Protectors.
I think how sacred they
are to our way of life,
to staying alive, as I float
just out of their reach. I feel
the burden, the duty,
the heaviness of carrying water
to crops, to livestock,
to the garden patch.

it was the knowledge
that it added time + agony
to our own days and nights,
not theirs, that we feared

Sometimes the weight of my own
water is too heavy to carry alone.
Emotions flow through us,
fill our vessels, escape
our eyes as water droplets,
lift as rainbow against autumn sky.

one asked for milk;
how he longed for the sweetness
of the taste.
the connection
of being joined
to his mother
didn't cross our minds
until he was gone

I remember the joy of carrying
my children, filled with their own water,
inside of me. And then my water
broke. They carried their water
forward, away from me.
They were able to live because
of breastmilk I made from my water.

it was then
we realized
it would not have
made a difference
in his pneumonia;
in anything except
a small pleasure
we had no right to deny

I watch as the Water Protectors
are hurt by their water,
our water,
as it is used,
a weapon,
against them.

Today She Told Me

she'd felt like a tool,
an old car
that served a purpose
of getting them—her dad, an uncle,
her tennis coach—
from one destination
to another,
but like that old junker car
she wasn't cared for,
didn't have any value or worth,
was dispensable,
easily tossed aside and forgotten
when she no longer
served a purpose;
that of allowing them
to jack off in her mouth
with no consideration
of the damage that was done,
that would never be undone,
until 40 years later,
after her husband died
and their two sons were grown,
a neighbor man
held her
in front of a mirror,
told her to look at herself,
see her beauty and her value;
that day she took a deep breath,
felt alive
for the first time
shiny and new.

In Waves

the rain does thrash
against window pane
as wind bends bough
of willow, grass and
human form. Break
the wave from sound
upon the shore
to heal this wrath upon
our earth, to reside
in silence yet once more.

Still the heart that pummels inside,
"So wild, too fast," I cried.
"I need time to live and love,
to hold my child against my bosom,
to speak with the man I love in wisdom,
to repent the sins I have committed!"

But it was time, my eyes did close,
moving chest at rest.
The wave did come within the night,
and,
finally,
I had my quiet.

Publication Notes

Some of the poems in this book were previously published in the following publications. A special thank you to those editors who chose them.

Website: *Heartland! Poets of Love, Resistance & Solidarity*
"We Stand" - February 4, 2017.
"Geese" – June 21, 2017

Tittynope Zine, second edition – 2017
"Inverted Tulips"
"If you Want"
"Geese"
"We Stand"

365 Days, A Poetry Anthology: The 365 Day Poets – August 3, 2016
"In Waves"
"Winter Meets"
"Each Day"
"I Wash"
"Green Tomatoes"

Gimme Your Lunch Money: Heartland Poets Speak out against Bullies (Paladin Contemporaries Scottsdale, Arizona, Kansas City, Missouri, 2016)
"Among the Wild Prime Rose"
"Born to Bully"
"EveryThing They Had"

I-70 Review - 2016
"Inverted Tulips"

Lawrence Journal World, World Company
"A Child Asks, What is Death?" 05/17/2015
"Still, I Wait" 08/09/2015
"I've Never Met a Muslim" 12/13/2015

Ronda Miller

Acknowledgments

Several people stand out in my mind when I think of the compilation and completion of *WaterSigns*. There are those authors who lent their time and expertise to reading *WaterSigns*, in a less than perfect format, to gift it with a descriptive blurb. I thank Kim Stafford, Denise Low, Kevin Rabas, Roy Beckemeyer, Tyler Sheldon, Al Ortolani, and Alan Kleiman for their time, kindness, creative words, and encouragement. I thank Mark Wolfson for his ongoing support, Caryn Mirriam-Goldberg for all she does for poetry and the human spirit, not to mention—me, and Marcia Epstein for accepting voice, even before grief has allowed it to form words.

Once in a great while, the human eye connects with an image that matches the vision of the inner eye. Crystal Socha's photography does that for me. Not only does her photography match the emotion and words in many of my poems, it inspires me to write additional poems. I can't thank her enough for her generous gifting of photographs to use on the cover and different sections within. As *WaterSigns* goes to print, I have yet to meet Crystal in person. Crystal has donated her time to transform several photographs into black and white versions for better printing results.

I'd like to thank Kansas Authors Club members for their support and friendship. They have provided me with numerous offerings of help, guidance, encouragement, and understanding. The poets who continue to offer titles and poetic postings and comments on James Benger's online Facebook site, 365 Days, are a driving force behind many of the poems on these pages. All of them first appeared in part or fully on his site.

Rarely does an author feel as confident in their publisher and editor as I continue to with Meadowlark Books and Tracy Million Simmons. I know that my book will be edited to perfection. Tracy is open to accepting, and sharing of, creative thoughts and ideas. She also critiques and corrects in a gentle, straight forward, easy to understand manner. She even uses humor! She once made a side note that American English speaking people do indeed use punctuation marks inside quotation marks! Tracy is an author's dream come true. I hope to work with her on numerous projects and genre in the future.

About the Author

Ronda Miller is a Life Coach who works with clients who have lost someone to homicide. She is a graduate of the University of Kansas and continues to live in Lawrence. She is a Fellow of The Citizen Journalism Academy, World Company, a Certified Life Coach with IPEC (Institute of Professional Empowerment Coaching), a mother to two step sons, Sasha and Nick, a son, Scott and a daughter, Apollonia. She created poetic forms loku and ukol. She was the co-chair, along with Caryn Mirriam-Goldberg, for the Transformative Language Arts Conference at Unity Village September, 2015. Miller was the poetry contest manager for Kansas Authors Club (2011-2014). She is the District 2 President of Kansas Authors Club (2015 – 2017), and the club's Vice President (2016 – 2017). When Miller isn't coaching clients, volunteering time to Kansas Authors Club, or writing poetry, she is busy learning life skills from children with special needs.

*Author Photos by Karen Ledford

Special Thanks to

Crystal Socha

whose photographs are poetry in visual form

About the Photographs

Crystal Socha started her photography career with a 4x5 large format camera. She developed and printed all of her own photographs. Although she still shoots with her film camera, she has made the transition to the digital age.

Crystal primarily focuses on landscapes, but over the last couple of years has developed a love of photographing eagles and other wildlife. She enjoys spending time in the Flint Hills of Kansas capturing not only its vast rolling landscape, but also the ranching life, which unfolds in the heart of the hills.

When Crystal isn't out photographing she spends her time taking care of her horses. She has also driven and trained Belgian hitch horses for competition. She's done that for fifteen years, winning several team classes. She is currently driving a team of horses at the Cowtown Museum in Wichita, Kansas.

fineartamerica.com/profiles/crystal-socha.html
facebook.com/crystalsochaphotography/

Ronda Miller

Also by Ronda Miller

Going Home: Poems from My Life (April 2012)

MoonStain (Meadowlark, May 2015)

Ronda's work can also be found in:

365 Days, A Poetry Anthology, edited by Roy Beckemeyer, James Benger, Dan Pohl, and Diane Wahto (CreateSpace, 2016)

Begin Again, 150 Kansas Poems, edited by Caryn Mirriam-Goldberg (Woodley Press, 2011)

Gimme Your Lunch Money: Heartland Poets Speak out against Bullies, edited by Dennis Etzel, Jr. and Lindsey Martin-Bowen (Paladin Contemporaries, 2016)

Kansas Time & Place, An Anthology of Heartland Poetry, edited by Roy J. Beckemeyer and Caryn Mirriam-Goldberg (Little Balkans Press, 2017)

To the Stars Through Difficulties, a Kansas Renga in 150 Voices, edited by Caryn Mirriam-Goldberg (Mammoth Publications, 2012)

View from Smoky Hill, Voices of the Plains: Poetry and Stories, album (Smoky Hill, 2015)

Co-author, "The 150th Reride of the Pony Express." (2010)

Poem, "Renunciation," can be found at The Smithsonian Art Institute Archives with artist Roger Shimomura's personal papers.

Ronda Miller

Also by Meadowlark Books

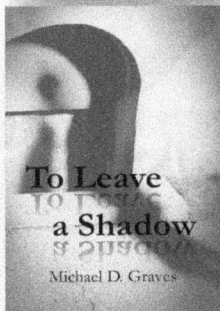

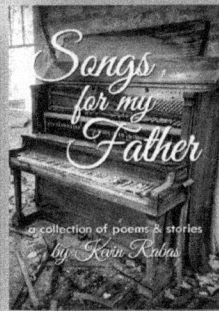

www.ingramcontent.com/pod-product-compliance
Lightning Source LLC
Chambersburg PA
CBHW020945090426
42736CB00010B/1277